How Does a Flower Grow?

Especially for my sister, Peggy Ribbons,
and for Hywel and Rachel Phillips

How Does a Flower Grow?

Jan Godfrey
Illustrated by D'reen Neeves

One day Billy Bear and Grandpa Bear planted seeds.
Grandpa Bear showed Billy Bear
how to poke the seeds into little holes in the earth.
The seeds were small and stripey and brown.

"How will they turn into flowers?" asked Billy Bear.
"You wait and see," said Grandpa Bear.
"Meanwhile we'll give the seeds a drink from your red watering-can."

It was fun watering the seeds, but it was hard to wait and see.
Early next morning Billy Bear went out into the garden.
He dug up the seeds with his blue trowel to see if they had grown.
The seeds were still there, small and stripey and brown.

Billy Bear was disappointed.
He pushed all the seeds back into their holes.
Just then a worm popped up.
"How does a flower grow?" Billy Bear asked the worm.

"I'm not too sure," said the worm.
"I work under the ground, wriggling to keep it all nice and fresh-airy.
Your seeds need that."
Before Billy Bear could blink, the worm popped down its hole.

Grandpa Bear said, "Now we must leave the seeds alone for a while."
"But how will the flowers grow?" asked Billy Bear.
"I need porridge to make me grow. Do seeds need porridge?"
"No," said Grandpa.
"Seeds need soil and water and air and rain and warm sunshine.
Then God makes tiny roots grow down and tiny shoots grow up."

So every day Billy Bear watered the seeds with his red watering-can.
And the sun shone and the rain rained
and the worm wriggled and the seeds began to grow.

Then one morning Billy Bear looked in the garden.
There were tiny plants with green stalks and green leaves.
"Hooray," shouted Billy Bear. "But where are the flowers?"

Billy Bear met a snail.

The snail was walking very… very… slowly.

"How *does* a flower grow?" asked Billy Bear sadly.

"Slowly…" said the snail. "Plants… are… slow… just… like… me…
No… use… hurrying… us."

And the snail moved… slowly… away…

"Your seeds are growing nicely," said Grandpa Bear.
"But you must still wait and see."
So Billy Bear went on waiting and the plants went on growing.

They grew taller and taller and taller until…
they were as tall as Billy Bear…
The worm and his friends looked out of their holes.
"That's a big plant," said the worms.

They went on growing taller and taller until they were…
as tall as Grandpa Bear.
The butterflies came to see the plant.
They fluttered in and out of the leaves.

Then one day Billy Bear looked in the garden.
There were lots of big, beautiful, yellow flowers.
The flowers looked like the sun.
They had golden petals and friendly faces.
The bees liked the flowers very much.
They hummed and buzzed at Billy Bear.

"There you are," said Grandpa Bear to Billy Bear.
"They are called sunflowers."
Billy Bear wondered and wondered.
Could God possibly make sunflowers out of tiny seeds,
with only the sun and the rain
and the soil and a red watering-can and a blue trowel
and a wriggling worm to help him?
"You're very clever, God," said Billy Bear.

A Tamarind Book
Published in association with SU Publishing
130 City Road, London EC1V 2NJ
ISBN 1 873824 21 1

First edition 1993
First paperback edition 1995

Printed and bound in Singapore